The All-New Dieter's Guide to Weight Loss During Sex

The All-New Dieter's Guide to Weight Loss During Sex

by Richard Smith

Workman Publishing
New York

Library of Congress Cataloguing-in-Publication Data

Smith, Richard
    The all-new dieter's guide to weight loss during sex by Richard Smith.
        p.   cm.
    ISBN 1-56305-781-6
    1. Sex—Humor. 2. Weight loss—Humor. I. Title.
PN6231.S54S562   1995
818'.5407—dc20   94-47003
                                                                      CIP

Workman books are available at special discounts when purchased in bulk for premiums and sales promotions as well as for fund-raising or educational use. Special editions or book excerpts can also be created to specification. For details, please contact the Special Sales Director at the address below.

Workman Publishing
708 Broadway
New York, NY 10003-9555

Manufactured in the United States of America

10 9 8 7 6 5 4 3 2 1

For L.B., who double-checked each calorie.

Contents

III. Lite Sex 29

IV. Foreplay 39

V. Going All the Way 53

VI. Orgasm, and Beyond 77

VII. Afterplay.............................91

VIII. Supplementary Pleasures..105

IX. Sex-Related Stress.............117

X. Family Values 131

The All-New Dieter's Guide to Weight Loss During Sex

(Just when you thought all the good exercises were taken.)

Introduction

The scientific basis for weight loss during sex was first explored in the original *Dieter's Guide to Weight Loss During Sex,* an exercise program on which over 1,000,000 dieters lost a total of nearly 8 pounds.

Since then, women have grown more demanding and men have gotten heavier. In addition, new weight loss breakthroughs, including laser technology and cold fusion, have enabled researchers to more precisely determine not only calories burned during sex, but which calories—thigh, tummy or hips. Our bedside computer, with its fiber-optic sensors, enabled us to calculate weight loss to the nearest calorie, even for low-impact sexual activities such as moaning, dabbing away tears of joy and checking one's voice mail. Indeed, our test couples had nothing but praise for this program, and testimonials such as "More fun than our visit to EPCOT" (Ramona and Trigger, newlyweds) and "Wow, at last I can wear a bikini" (Tammy, philosopher) were not uncommon.

Conscientious dieters will be happy to learn that several of our new weight loss categories reflect an increased appreciation of the benefits of sexual activity, especially by multi-taskers who rely on sex not only for reproduction but also to a) relieve stress, b) act as an exercise supplement (studies show that women over 40 who have firm upper arms make love 17 or more times a week, rain or shine), c) reverse the aging process and, if lovemaking is sufficiently vigorous, d) function as both a moisturizer *and* night repair gel.

Furthermore, to ensure accuracy, our couples were studied under actual lovemaking conditions. For warm-weather sex, participants performed on vibrating beach chairs in Malibu, their only protection from the sun an application of tanning lotion (SPF 30) and two surfers waving palm fronds. To determine cold-weather weight loss, our test couple spent the month of February in a cabin in Bemidji, Minnesota, where our researchers put ice cubes down their back. And, for calories consumed during sex under unusual circumstances, our subjects made love in their bedroom.

NEW HOPE FOR LAPSED LOVERS

Couples who are "rusty" may at first find many of the exercises daunting, particularly those calling for a "practice" good-night kiss and "hands-on" sex. Not to worry. Our research shows that even the most out-of-practice lovers (two-career couples and individuals addicted to golf), when they resumed where they had left off, needed no more than 3.2 minutes to recall the basics and only another 4 minutes to implement advanced skills.*

WHY DOES THIS DIET WORK?

Why shouldn't it? Not surprisingly, our researchers found that 1) unlike other diets, feelings of deprival are minimal, and 2) it provides for the four basic food groups plus salsa. In addition and despite the misgivings of several unregistered nutritionists, we feel the effectiveness of *Dieter's Guide* is due in no small part to its aversion to rigidity: lovers are permitted to eat corn on the cob during foreplay—a first!

IS THIS WEIGHT LOSS PROGRAM FOR EVERYONE?

Yes, especially couples who:
1. Wish to strengthen their relationship.
2. Want to stay in shape by staying home.
3. Prefer the intimacy of their bedroom to the glare of a gym.

Extreme Sports Note: In calculating weight loss, only normal sexual activities, the kind that can be done at home, have been included. This does not, however, preclude an adventurous couple from experimenting with activities they feel will accelerate weight loss. Reports from couples rave about the efficacy of sex in space ("Totally awesome!"—Juan and Gigi, space shuttle stowaways; "Ever

---

*Lab studies of recovering divorcees deprived of sex for up to 48 hours confirm this.

so spiritual!"—Myrtle and Barney, tai chi instructors), and those on the cutting edge of passion will think nothing of, in their quest for weight loss, making love while calculating their retirement benefits.

WHAT IS SAFE SEX?

Something we stress throughout *Dieter's Guide*. For new lovers it means using a protective device, such as a condom or a stern chaperone. For couples with curious children, it means locking the bedroom door. And for the weary housewife, safe sex can be either keeping her apron fastened or feigning sleep when she feels something go bump in the night.

THE BIGGEST QUESTION OF ALL

How long will it take to reach my weight loss goal? The answer is, who knows? An intensely active honeymoon couple, after a mere weekend on The Diet, might find on Monday morning that they've lost enough weight to pass through a napkin ring. The two-career couple, on the other hand, forced to have sex while commuting, may take up to 6 years just to shed 2 pounds.

I. In Quest of a Partner

Finding that one special person for caring, sharing and wonderful sex is not always easy. Happily for dieters, trying to meet someone you actually want to sleep with, even if you have access to the Internet, can burn thousands of calories. The horror of a bad blind date (defined as one who shows up with his Yorkie in an infant carrier) can burn over 700 calories and pare down those love handles that make you think twice about bicycle pants. And one woman instantly shed three pounds when, on the second date, a man she considered a "possible" confessed he still lived at home . . . and shared a bedroom with his mother.

In the following pages you will see not only why the search for a lover causes weight loss, but how, once you've met a partner, those first initial intimacies—holding hands, gazing into each other's eyes across candlelight dinners, fighting for the clicker, even carving a jack-o'-lantern together—permit weight loss to continue.

Note: Even if you already have a partner, study this section to determine retroactive weight loss.

Close Encounters

There are many ways to meet the perfect partner. One man, as he was leaving a restaurant, captured the heart of the woman at the next table by thrusting his business card in her chicken salad. And a Georgia state trooper, when it comes to meeting cute guys, swears by her speed traps. Unfortunately, meeting terrific partners doesn't burn calories. Trying to survive a series of losers, on the other hand, can burn up to 300 calories per encounter, even more if they're needy.* Extra calories are burned if you're a magnet for any of the following:

Activity	Calories Burned
Rejects from singles bars . . . . .22 *(Add 15 calories if they show up wearing several gold chains around their neck.)*	
Rejects from leather bars . . . . .62 *(Add 72 calories if they're wearing any kind of chain.)*	
Perky women . . . . .9 (Weigh only 8 pounds, always feel a draft.)	
Geeky men . . . . .100 (Use pocket protectors, wear their pants too high.)	

*Immediately ask you out for New Year's Eve, and it's only July.

Bad Signs

(Indications that this is not the person you want to bring home to mother.)

Activity	Calories Burned
He's wearing rings:	
One nose	.19
Two eyebrow	.22
Three navel	.34
And a pinkie ring	.51
She's wearing lots of makeup	.26
It's flaking into her soup	.70
She's speed-reading "Victory over Migraines"	.37
He's lip-reading "Mercenary"	.60
(Add 6 calories if he's choking back tears.)	
He's sitting with a chaperone	.11
A bodyguard	.55
His tailor	.90

The Blind Date

One of the more anxiety-inducing events, especially if your aunt insists he has a great personality (the kiss of death). Look on the bright side, however; even if there's no chemistry, you may make a new friend—he could turn out to be that special someone who'll feed your cat when you're away. Happily, the worse the experience, the more calories you burn.

Activity	Calories Burned
Meeting for dinner:	
In a restaurant	.11
That isn't dark enough	.28
If he constantly makes cellular calls:	
To business associates	.9
To Dial-A-Mattress	.99
Makes an unauthorized sexual advance:	
Puts a hand on your knee	.41
Promises you a recording contract	.12
Tastes your swordfish steak	.60
Removes food lodged between his teeth:	
With a toothpick	.10
With a magnet	.84
By violently shaking his head	.220
Talks only about sports	.20
Saving the earth	.31
How God loves you	.42
(Subtract 6 calories if you already knew this.)	
His last relationship	.200

Weight Loss Bonus #1

Activity	Calories Burned
He has his credit card rejected	18

And you have to:	
Pay	25
Wash dishes	37
Return the meal	400

One Last Hurdle

He wants to come in for a nightcap	10
You're too timid to say no	55
Waiting outside your apartment until he finishes his drink	187

Losing Hope

After a series of grim evenings, deciding that you'll never meet that special someone can be dangerous. You might even do something desperate, like sign up for a singles weekend in the Catskills. Fortunately, there are alternatives:

Activity	Calories Burned
Joining a self-help group	11
Joining a self-pity group	35
Turning to the personals	15
Village Voice	28
New York Review of Books	40
(Avoid particularly any ad with the phrase "soul of a poet." It means his sheets haven't been changed since Irangate.)	
The phone book	200
Turning to God	14
Because of your faith	5
Because it's cheaper	73

Regaining Hope

Defined as that moment when you stop calling friends to complain that there are no good men out there. Calorie counts indicate weight lost when you finally meet someone who is:

Activity	Calories Burned
Gorgeous	.25
(30-calorie bonus if you're seen together by your far-less-gorgeous ex.)	
Courteous (opened the car door for you)	.33
Smart (knew how to get a good table)	.37
Charming (the waitress brought extra-large portions)	.44
Presumptuous (brought an overnight bag)	.271

Five things to do when the right lover comes along:

1. Rejoice.

2. Dump the wrong one.

3. Be sorry you got that tattoo.

4. Wear diaphanous underwear (to better enable partner to see your inner soul).

5. Buy a new shower curtain.

Breaking the Ice

When you finally meet someone with partner-potential, you'll know it. You'll walk on air. You'll neglect your friends. And those first innocent touches will make you tingle— if she doesn't push your hand away.

Activity	Calories Burned
Taking long, romantic walks	.20
If you forgot your orthotics	.55
Taking his arm because:	
You're possessive	.16
You're training him	.29
It's a sneaky way to check for mushy biceps	.55
Gazing into each other's eyes	.5
If there's chemistry	.92
Playfully tousling his hair	.17
If he doesn't have any	.80
Spreading a coat over a puddle when she steps from the curb	.11
While she's wearing it	.85

Public Displays of Affection

Showing the world that "we are an item" is not only sexy, but a universal form of safe sex (unless, of course, you're seen by busybodies). Some of the more popular aspects:

Activity	Calories Burned
Sharing an umbrella	12
From a piña colada	56
Blowing kisses at each other (per kiss)	3
Wind with you	5
Wind against you	40
Nuzzling on a park bench	19
If you're oblivious to passersby	28
If you're oblivious to the "Wet Paint" sign	63
Holding hands	8
To remind her she's yours	15
To remind him you still don't have an engagement ring	80
Spray-painting "I love Shirley" all over town	47
Getting arrested	520

Asking Permission to Go Further

This may diminish spontaneity, but if you're with a litigious partner it makes safe sex even safer.

Activity	Calories Burned
Clearing your throat	10
If you're nervous	24
Turning on tape recorder:	
To preserve this special moment	6
To protect yourself	9
(You may someday run for public office.)	
Asking partner if you may:	
Engage in fondling (lite)	11
Engage in fondling (heavy)	22
Carry his or her books	10
If partner a lit major	45
If partner a phys ed major	3
Dance closer	9
(Add 50 calories if her boyfriend's trying to cut in.)	
Slip into something comfortable	26
Slip out of something comfortable	55
(Add 10 calories if your voice cracks.)	
If partner answers no to all questions	66
Begging	123

Awkward Moments

Activity	Calories Burned
That first good-night kiss	.15
That second good-night kiss	.22
If things are going well	.75
Coming up for air	.5
If she won't let you	.39

Note: The man who starts worrying about whether or not she'll let him kiss her good night while they're still at the restaurant almost never adds up the dinner check.

Seducing Partner (Indirect)

For women, this is easy. A show of erotic force like a plunging neckline or explaining how his Macintosh works can have the strongest male pleading for Milk Duds. Men must try harder. Some can't-fail methods for both sexes:

Activity	Calories Burned
Telling her about your dysfunctional childhood	15
If she holds you close and comforts you	27
If she gives you her therapist's phone number	79
Quoting poetry:	
William Wordsworth	18
Sylvia Plath	155
Serenading her	17
From beneath her window	21
If the neighbors complain	99
Dancing to Gershwin	21
Dipping	42
Dropping her	75
Playing doctor	30
If you're not a health-care professional	200

Seducing Partner (Direct)

Instead of wasting the evening on dinner, a show, discussing world peace, the endangered rain forest, Serbia's emerging strongman, Camus, past relationships, what you want out of life and how two people should really get to know each other before having sex:

Activity	Calories Burned
Simply asking, "Do you want to go to bed?" 11
Getting slapped 376

Stalling for Time

It's fun to smooch, but you're not quite ready for sex. Perhaps you need more time. Or you want to consult a psychic friend. Some diplomatic remarks to use when declining sex:

Activity	Calories Burned
Let's get to know each other better	14
My mother's waiting up for me	20
I have a big day tomorrow. I'm:	
Taking the bar exam	27
Getting married	93
Getting my cat spayed	146
I'm saving myself for:	
The right one	18
Prom night	50
It's not the right time:	
I'm still getting over my ex	39
My parents are in the back seat	83
I'm not dressed for it:	
Wearing frayed underwear	27
Not wearing a condom	78
I forget how	84

Playing Hard to Get

Activity	Calories Burned
If partner persistent	.32
Gently pushing him away	.55
Gently pushing his tongue away	.5
With a snow shovel	.70
Holding out for the right moment	.27
Holding out for the right ring:	
2 karats	.81
5 karats	.133
Playing harder to get	.175

Just Saying No

Activity	Calories Burned
If he's:	
Resistible (you're head still rules your heart)	10
Irresistible (your heart's starting to win)	50
If she's:	
A "ten"	28
Blowing in your ear	35
And your libido's the size of Belgium	257
If it's been 7 months since:	
You've been with someone	20
Your divorce	39
Your messy divorce	56
If it's your wedding night	400

Biggest Lie Told by Singles

Activity	Calories Burned
"I really like my freedom." *	11

*Pertains particularly to:

Women who . . .	Men who . . .
Own two or more cats	Live within their means
Depend on their brother-in-law to fix them up	Depend on their sister-in-law to trim their hair
Cry at bridal showers	Toast New Year's Eve by clinking their glass against a mirror
Are always the first to arrive	Are always the last to leave

Sex-Free Sex

Activity	Calories Burned
Conservative cuddling	.16
Shaking hands good night	.6
High fives	.12
Respectful rubbing	.17
Frantic groping	.40
Moderate ogling (per ogle)	.3
Restrained petting (above the eyebrows)	.11
Gentle teasing	.13
Exchanging recipes	.14
Leading each other on	.8
For years	.245
Staring longingly at each other	.9
Through binoculars	.50
Drinks at Disneyland	.10

II. Preparing for Sex

When at last you meet that special someone (or a reasonable facsimile), begin with a romantic setting—one that makes your lover hope, unless your air conditioner broke, that the night will never end.

Examine the bathroom. Does it sparkle? Can you eat salad off the floor? When it comes to romance, aesthetics matter—is there a new cake of soap in the sink, or that pathetic chip of Ivory you've been hoarding till payday? Make sure the refrigerator's stocked—a partner deprived of leftovers is useless. And a decent microwave can't hurt. Popcorn is lover-friendly and low in calories.

Inspect the bedroom. Do soiled sweatsocks litter the floor? Is it too late to take up that shag carpeting? If you have lots of disposable income, strew the bed with orchids. If you don't, a few stuffed animals will do. Change the sheets, fluff the pillows and, if your last partner was partial to hair pomade, change the pillowcases. Check under the bed. Dustballs and crumpled tissues will repulse a finicky partner.

Finally, be considerate: are there novels on tape or magazines for your partner to flip through should you take too long in the bathroom to arrange yourself? (Studies show that restless men, while waiting for their partner to emerge from the bathroom, have actually gotten their masters in business administration.) For now, concentrate on getting ready for lovemaking—and creating an environment that puts you both at ease. (*Note:* If you're feeling slightly anxious, just imagine what Martha Stewart would do.)

Bedside Basics

Things no lover's night table should be without:

Item	Purpose
Tissues	Dab away tears of joy
Flashlight	Assist in after-sex search for earring, contact lens, partner
Phone	If you like to kiss and tell
Bottled water	To pour on overheated partner
Hand mirror	Reality check—if you fog it up, sex is going well
Floor plan	To guide partner from bedroom to bathroom in middle of the night
"Save the Whales" poster	Indicates sensitivity
Bowl of M&M's	For strength
Bowl of condoms	For luck
Braid of garlic	To ward off visitors

The Romantic Bathroom

Not an oxymoron if it has a) indirect lighting and b) no kitty litter under the sink.

Activity	Calories Burned
Boiling the bath mat	33
Exchanging high-mileage towels for fluffy new ones*	19
Discarding a previous lover's toothbrush	2
Waterpik	9
Making certain there's a full roll of toilet paper	5
Reading material	11
Glade (raspberry scent)	8
Removing embarrassing items from medicine cabinet:	
Prozac	6
Bulk laxative (Metamucil)	9
Bulky laxative (Shredded Wheat)	12
Grecian Formula	8
Anti-gas tablets (regular)	4
Anti-gas tablets (nerve)	61
Suppositories	12
L-shaped	94
Removing damp panty hose from towel rack:	
Hers	8
His	152

*A towel is "high-mileage" when you can see through it.

The Romantic Bedroom

Converting a ho-hum room into a temple of lust is easier than you think. It might mean doing something simple, like placing fresh flowers by the bed or, if there's an allergy problem, a bowl of Pringles. Additional touches:

Activity	Calories Burned
Discarding empty beer cans	9
If you've grown emotionally attached to them	55
Changing the sheets	22
Just wringing them out	38
Hiding your good jewelry	25
(until you know your partner better)	
Repositioning the bed (for a better view of the moon):	
King-size bed	78
Sleigh bed	94
With partner already in it	147
Affixing "Thank you for not smoking" notice to headboard	10
Dimming the lights for ambience	4
To conceal peeling wallpaper	12
Lighting candles for intimacy	6
To keep warm	22
Watering the fern	10
Setting place card on each pillow	2

The Details

If the mood is right, even the most tone-deaf partner will suddenly hear gypsy violins (quite a feat if you're playing Engelbert Humperdinck). Some further tips to ensure a memorable evening:

Activity	Calories Burned
Getting rid of nonessential items:	
Your baby blanket	15
If this causes anxiety	30
Ratty bunny slippers	11
Spare motorcycle parts	46
That photo of you and your ex in a hot tub	22
Getting rid of nonessential personnel:	
Your hamster	5
Your roommate	155
Loading the CD player with:	
Chopin (*Add 12 calories per nocturne.*)	20
Nine Inch Nails	52
Yanni	2
Lowering your answering machine	5
(So your partner doesn't hear a message beginning, "You really tired me out last night.")	
Checking your electronic organizer to make sure it's the right night	19
Drawing the shades	8
If the neighbors object	50

Buying Condoms*

Standing before the "Family Planning Center" at the drugstore, trying to be an informed consumer and decide which condom is appropriate, can burn more calories than a week at tennis camp, especially if you're recognized. The choices are overwhelming, there's that feeling that everyone is watching you, and even more calories are burned if, when you go to pay, the cashier says, "I know what you're going to do."

Activity	Calories Burned
Putting on sunglasses	.3
Considering the choices	.11
Trying to appear nonchalant	.25
Whistling	.37
Making a selection:	
If you're uninhibited	.4
Self-conscious	.55
Not sure of your size	.108
Asking advice from salesclerk	.17
Who turns out to be your girlfriend's father	.1,000
Coping with embarrassment	.92
(Cashier holds up your 10-pack of Trojans and shouts, "I need a price!")	
Getting fitted	.308

*Wise lovers save money by buying in bulk.

Creating a Diversion

(Condom-buying strategies for those who live in a small town.)

Activity	Calories Burned
Purchasing decoy items:	
Aspirin	.9
Hair conditioner	.11
Mother's Day card	.14
Bathroom scale	.29
Tums	.5
Cough drops	.6
Valium	.18
Without a prescription	.70
Barney cassette	.13

Primping (Her)

Activity	Calories Burned
Tweezing stray facial hairs	.3
Applying false eyelashes	.15
While driving to partner's house	.129
Assembling the perfect outfit	.25
One your partner can remove easily	.4
One that makes you look five years younger	.41
If the cleaners was closed	.192
Discovering a last-minute zit	.8
Cursing it	.3
Popping it	.22
Checking breath with hand	.4
With neighbor	.30
Applying deodorant:	
Spray	.3
Roll-on	.12
Mentally preparing yourself with:	
Eastern philosophy (zen)	.5
Western philosophy (karaoke)	.51
Striking a pose in front of the mirror	.8
Flexing	.65

Grooming (Him)

Activity	Calories Burned
Sucking in	.24

When Is It Appropriate to Have Sex?

After 5 dates? 10 dates? Before your roommate gets home? Because he or she brought you fresh flowers, paid for dinner and the movie, treated you to popcorn (jumbo container), bought you a teddy bear and didn't ask for gas money doesn't mean you're obligated to have sex.*

Activity	Calories Burned
Waiting until marriage	.18
If your hormones are raging	.371
Waiting until dark	.2

*Instead of immediately sleeping with each other, conservative experts suggest suppressing the sexual urge by just napping a little.

III. Lite Sex

You're through preparing. Your partner's references check out, the question of "your place or mine?" has been resolved (generally, the partner with either the best address or the fewest dirty dishes in the sink plays host), and you're ready to go further. Even if you desperately want each other, however, take your time. Slowly removing each other's clothes and folding them neatly burns far more calories then simply tearing them off and doing a swan dive into the bed. Instead, sitting on the couch and quietly holding hands until your cat retires for the night will, when you finally do have sex, make it that much better. And communicate. Get even closer to each other by sharing political views or, more creative, exchanging contour maps of your erogenous zones.

If you think, once you touch each other, things are going to escalate, now may be a good time to:

- Set the alarm
- Open the champagne
- Close the drapes

Making That First Move

Activity	Calories Burned
If you're bold and confident	2
If you're like the rest of us	455

Sexual Ethics

What no principled lover should be without. Now is the appropriate time to confess that you:

Activity	Calories Burned
Still have your virginity	19
And you're on your third divorce	271
Snore	11
During sex	58
Hog the blankets	15
Look different without:	
Your hairpiece	19
Your teeth	40
Your Elvis outfit	75
Lied about your age by 2 years	17
By 15 years	29
Had corrective surgery:	
Face lift	20
Fanny lift	35
Tummy tuck	40
Chemical peel	22
Sex change	149
Underwent breast enlargement using:	
A surgeon	42
A Wonderbra	90
Have poison ivy	85
Grind your teeth	7

Getting Your Partner's Attention

Indicating that you want to make love should be a sensitive, sweet gesture. It may be a secret signal, such as dropping a hankie on the floor, or discreetly nuzzling her neck and announcing, "Attention K-Mart Shopper!" If partner's dense, or dozing on the couch, something more drastic may be called for, like gently tossing pebbles at his fly. Additional methods:

Activity	Calories Burned
Wiggling your eyebrows	7
Batting your eyelashes	11
Sitting in partner's lap	16
If partner using laptop	76
Beckoning partner with little finger	5
With grappling hook	40
Dismissing butler for the night	6
Calling partner by pet name	19
If dog comes running over	62
Just throwing yourself at partner	22
Missing	100

Affirmative Action

Activity	Calories Burned
Letting partner know you want to "get together" tonight	32

Places to Leave a Note

For him:	For her:
TV screen	Makeup mirror
Wallet	Purse
Golf bag	Gym bag
Windshield of car	Screen of favorite ATM machine
Lunch pail	Briefcase
Sports page of evening paper	Reading glasses
Six-pack	Mud pack
Shoulder bag	Shoulder holster

Note: Post-its can be placed anywhere (her forehead, his adam's apple) and are available in a variety of colors to match your partner's eyes.

Kissing*

The details:

Activity	Calories Burned
Removing chewing gum	.5
Puckering up	.2
If lips are chapped	.15
Shutting eyes	¼
Peeking to see if partner's are shut, too	.4
French kissing (tongues touch)	.32
Italian kissing (tongues knot)	.50
American kissing (tongues wag)	.83
Air kisses because:	
You're still getting to know each other	.14
You're nine inches taller	.62

*Safe sex if you only rub noses.

Hickey

Activity	Calories Burned
If only the two of you see it 4	
If everyone at work sees it 752	

Getting Personal

Busy lovers often omit this phase, preferring instead to warm up their partner in a microwave.

Activity	Calories Burned
Kneading partner's neck muscles	17
Licking partner all over	25
Swallowing partner's earring	9
If it's real gold	15
And partner wants it back	392
Blowing softly on partner's toes:	
To arouse partner	17
To dry her nail polish	31
Driving partner up a wall	20
Flooring it	77

Arousal

At this point, if things are going well, you will suddenly find yourself indifferent to political reform.

Activity	Calories Burned
Clearing your mind of all negative thoughts	10
If the IRS is after you	152
Squirming	22
Getting antsy	35
Heavy breathing	50
Panting (per pant)	6
If you're asthmatic	52
Squeezing your partner's hand	12
Squeezing your rabbit's foot (for luck)	28
Holding your partner tighter	22
Crushing the sex manual	41
Writhing out of control	49
Conniptions	81

Getting into Bed

Gently leading your partner by the hand into the bedroom is nice, but it burns few calories. Using your partner as a free weight, on the other hand, can burn off that tuna melt you had for lunch.

Activity	Calories Burned
Carrying your partner into the bedroom	69
Carrying each other into the bedroom	418
Removing each other's slippers	11
Removing her nightie	16
Trying it on	58
Discussing what to do next	17
Lying down on:	
A water bed	14
An inner-spring mattress	19
An outer-spring mattress	174
A canopy bed	22
If you're claustrophobic	100

Note: Sex always goes better when the bed contains a marital aid, such as a dust ruffle.

IV. Foreplay

This is where the breathing gets heavy, so make sure the doors are locked.* If you need to use the bathroom, do so now. Those who respond to a partner's "God, don't stop now" with "I have to go powder my nose" should not expect a warm welcome when they return. (Unstable men find this sort of interruption particularly unsettling and may need several Tic Tacs to recapture the mood.) Foreplay activities will not just help you lose weight; they will arouse you even more. Don't be afraid to try new things. One formerly impotent lover achieved a remarkable recovery by watching his partner walk around the room wearing nothing but a cowbell (he was a dairy farmer). And a woman obsessed with gardening returned the sizzle to her love life by having sex in a wheelbarrow.

Four things to check for in your lover's bedroom:

1. Sufficient ventilation
2. Fitted sheets
3. Take-out menus
4. A hidden microphone

---

*If you're at a hotel, be certain the "Do not disturb" sign on the doorknob faces correctly. Displaying the "Please make up the room" side invites disaster.

Getting Undressed

Couples pressed for time usually toss their clothes in a heap, then curse themselves in the morning for not bringing a travel iron. (*Tip:* If he's going to bed with you for your mind, you need not undress.)

Activity	Calories Burned
Removing:	
Her bra	11
If you can't figure out how it opens	25
And she's not cooperating	80
Her skirt	16
Zipper stubborn	29
Zipper stuck	50
His jeans:	
Zipper fly	17
Button fly	33
Over his riding boots	75
His beeper	11
If he feels naked without it	20
Her badge	10
If she's on the vice squad	75
Her jewelry	16
If she's afraid you'll pawn it	88

Note: 10-calorie bonus if you remove her T-shirt without disturbing her cowboy hat.

If Partner Looked Better in Uniform*

Activity	Calories Burned
Army	.19
Navy	.25
Police:	
L.A.	.39
Muncie, Indiana	.5
Cleric	.87
Football	.154
Usher	.6
Majorette	.70
Lifeguard	.115

Point of Sexual Etiquette

No need to worry if you're nervous about those few extra pounds:
- They're difficult to see by candlelight.
- You look thinner when you're lying down.
- Most likely they'll come off during sex.

---

*The impact of seeing one's partner naked varies. Some women, if they like what they see, light an extra candle. Some men actually turn off the television set. And discovering she's gorgeous can cause a surprised male to burn 500 calories, then have a stroke.

Love at First Sight

Activity	Calories Burned
Penis envy:	
For man	.42
For woman	.19
For owner	.70
For Mr. Bobbit	.238

Warming Up Your Partner

This can range from a simple cuddle to, if you don't like what you see, putting his clothes back on. This is an important step, so take your time, even if you have theater tickets.

Activity	Calories Burned
Petting above the waist	.26
Petting below the waist	.59
Also using your free hand	.220
Slowly circling rim of partner's ear:	
With your tongue	.11
On your bicycle	.77
Kissing partner all over:	
Intensively (Your lips move, partner stays still.)	.48
Lazily (Your partner moves, your lips stay still.)	½
Just moving partner closer to radiator	.40

Maintaining Momentum

Activity	Calories Burned
Tossing another log on the fire	19
From across the room	50
Slow-dancing naked	3
Face to face	7
Cheek to cheek	41
Bringing out the beast in your partner	30
Putting it back in	100
Blowing in partner's ear	20
Both ears at once	139
Love bites:	
Of partner	8
Of prune danish (for extra energy)	15
Driving each other to ecstasy	32
Automatic	40
Stick shift	80

Losing Momentum

Activity	Calories Burned
Call of nature	134

Oral Sex*

Activity	Calories Burned
Flossing	18
Donning a lobster bib (finicky lovers only)	22
Psyching yourself	15
If you're afraid of losing face	118
Doing it	25
If you're inexperienced	31
Having trouble breathing	42
A vegetarian	130
The product of a strict Catholic upbringing	1
Kosher	92
If partner is talented	78
Has an overbite	136
Losing your place	4
Losing your retainer	269

*Unsafe sex if partner is teething.

Removing a Hair from Your Mouth

Don't worry if you can't. Unless it's dyed or moussed, the calories are negligible.

Activity	Calories Burned
Calling time out	.5
Trying to find it	.11
Trying to grab it	.14
With your pinkie	.26
With your partner's pinkie	.37
If it's elusive	.33
If it's wet	.61
Making those clicking sounds	.12
Using ice tongs (only as a last resort)	.51
If it's a chest hair	.9
With its follicle	.12
If it's a nose hair	.3
If it's a sideburn	.98
Discarding it on sheet	.5
On partner	.10
Framing it	.22
(appropriate only if it turns out to be your partner's first gray hair)	

Things Often Said During Foreplay

Activity	Calories Burned
Any original utterance	.21
A cliché	.6

Examples:

"Why'd you stop?"

"It's all in the wrist."

"I'm glad we skipped the party."

"Move down a little."

... "Too far, your feet are out the window."

"Am I too loud?"

"I love it when you yell."

"Please cover my mouth when I yawn."

"Is there film in the camera?"

"Could you possibly cash a check?"

"Leave the lights on, I have to watch my cholesterol."

"I can only stay the weekend."

"Dear Diary."

"You have a customer waiting."

Taking Responsibility for Your Own Pleasure

Activity	Calories Burned
Telling him what really turns you on	3
If you're shy	277
If he smiles knowingly	12
If he experiences cardiac arrest	249
Resuscitating him	114
Letting him turn blue	2

Note: When it comes to sex, men never speak up—they're grateful for anything.

Advanced Erogenous Zones

(For energetic lovers who've worn out the regular ones.)

Activity	Calories Burned
Busch Gardens:	
The tunnel of love	30
The water slide	97
A grassy hilltop under an azure sky:	
The Rockies	51
A putting green	8
Paris in the spring	63
Secaucus in the fall	11
A Hawaiian beach:	
With the person you came with	44
With the person you're leaving with	106
A romantic country inn:	
Owner leaves you alone	71
Owner keeps asking, "How's everything?"	5
A factory outlet:	
If you're turned on by your partner	127
If you're turned on by the bargains	300

Aromatherapy

A non-body-contact form of New Age sex.* This is an arousal technique specifically aimed at one of the more erotic shiatsu points on the body: the nose. Calorie counts indicate the degree of arousal by the partner doing the sniffing. Add 10 calories if your nose is stuffed.

Activity	Calories Burned
Sniffing:	
Her scented tissue	9
Her scented stationery:	
Love note	12
Chain letter	20
His scented after-shave:	
Brut	15
Aqua Velva	66
His scented sweatsocks	
(No calorie count—she didn't survive.)	
Her baking sticky buns	44
Burying your nose in her hair	6
Seconds after she sprayed it	28

*New Age sex is just like old age sex except, during climax, you chant "Om" instead of "Oy."

Why Have Sex?
(a Checklist)

Right Reasons	Wrong Reasons
Love	Lust*
Psychic friend said to	Psycho friend said to
Celebration: last mortgage payment	Celebration: last fling
Doctor's orders	Peer pressure
To satisfy your craving for sweets	Nothing good on TV
You've run out of conversation	You've run out of excuses
Your ex has the kids for the weekend	Your ex wants another chance
Nephews want a cousin	Baby-sitters need work
To lose weight	To lose your innocence
To keep up with your partner	To keep up with the Joneses
It's the perfect exercise	Can't afford health club dues

*A combination of love and lust is acceptable.

V. Going All the Way

"Love and commitment should precede all sex, unless they get in the way."

—*Swami Vishnu O'Brien*

Not just another weight loss gimmick but a vital expression of devotion—great sex on a regular basis (or irregular if your lover works odd hours) takes years off your face and adds years to your life. Besides working the entire body, intercourse burns up to 1,000 calories if both partners a) like to line-dance, and b) are in the same room.

Additionally, those who indulge report extraordinary side benefits such as:

- Fewer migraines
- More confidence when asking for a raise
- A decreased craving for couscous
- No wax buildup

First-Night Jitters (His)

Few aspects of sex afford so rich an opportunity for weight loss. The partner, for example, afflicted with a nervous stomach, whether caused by fear of failure or tainted borscht (tip: wash beets thoroughly), can count on a bonus of no fewer than 120 extra calories burned. A male partner made anxious by the sudden gleam in the eye of what he thought was a rather demure, even shy partner, especially if she's muttering, "Say your prayers, big boy," can expect to burn off at least 80 calories just working up the courage to remove his smoking jacket. Some typical problems:

Activity	Calories Burned
Feeling pressure to perform	15
She's reading you your rights	27
She's of noble birth	75
Rogaine not working	19
Working only on chest	75
She has bizarre sexual paraphernalia:	
A juicer	31
Matching pillowcases	110
To achieve the heights of ecstasy, she's using:	
Drugs	80
A forklift	116
She's a feminist	33
And earns more than you do	94

First-Night Jitters (Hers)

Thanks to NOW, this problem has been nearly eradicated.

Activity	Calories Burned
PMS	44
Bad hair day (He's not a natural blond.)	20
Forgiving him	13
He's much younger:	
Five years	7
Ten years	16
Still wearing his decoder ring	253
He keeps referring to bed as a work station	77
He thought *you* brought the condoms	36
He's using his fingers to count his sperm count	157

First-Night Jitters (Both)

Activity	Calories Burned
Forgot to drive the baby-sitter home 128	

Sex Education

Activity	Calories Burned
If you had it in school	.30
Flunked	.12
Got an A	.94
Taught	.200

The First Time

Activity	Calories Burned
Ever	115
(Add 92 calories if partner can tell.)	
Since last year	72
Since the collapse of the Soviet Union	382
Checking to see if it works	19
Checking for cobwebs	30

Couples without beginner's luck have their work cut out for them, especially if they clash astrologically. Hopefully, you're with an understanding partner, one who won't, if the earth doesn't move, immediately lose interest and resume adjusting the satellite dish.

The Second Time

Activity	Calories Burned
Discovering you're oversexed	.800

Inserting Diaphragm

Possible difficulties encountered by a nervous lover:

Activity	Calories Burned
If she does it	.18
If he does it	.572
If it pops out	.11
Chasing it	.57
Retrieving it from behind the bureau	.21
From your neighbor's bird feeder	.75

Putting on Condom

Eager lovers often have difficulty, especially if it's still in the package.* In extreme cases, the mood is totally destroyed and can be recaptured only by going back and starting the evening all over again (exhausting if you've already put in a full 10-hour workday). Following are activities most often associated with this phase of safe sex.

Activity	Calories Burned
Unwrapping condom	.11
If he's excited	.55
If she's impatient	.24
Snapping her fingers	.95
Applying condom:	
With erection	.7
Without erection	.484
Backwards	.600
Using assistance:	
His partner	.38
(Add 894 calories if she breaks a nail.)	
His valet	.66

*And package is marked "Official Use Only."

The Overeager Lover

Activity	Calories Burned
Putting on condom prematurely, while:	
Still in the restaurant	18
Buying flowers	30
Picking flowers	72
Caught in the evening rush hour:	
In your car	15
On public transportation	148
Ringing her doorbell	66
Very prematurely (while asking her out)	197

Point of Sexual Etiquette

Who pays for condoms? If it was good for both of you, split the cost. A woman who brought her own may demand a shipping and handling fee, but only after sex.

The Undereager Lover

Activity	Calories Burned
Putting on condom moments before orgasm 423	
Putting on condom moments after orgasm 7	

Intercourse

Activity	Calories Burned
If he takes his time 278	
If he's just like all the others 4	

The Stages

There are three official rates of speed: a) slow, b) idling, and c) "Wow!" For conscientious dieters, we offer a breakdown.

Activity	Calories Burned
Adjusting lumbar support	5
Beginning slowly and gently	12
Putting down novel	9
Getting in sync	18
Getting excited	27
Beginning to perspire	32
Picking up the pace	45
Without telling him	146
Losing control	71
Wild abandon	105
Demonic possession	179
Polaroid moment	300
Meltdown	3

Losing Erection

Activity	Calories Burned
Feeling around for it	.36

Reminder

It will be much easier to find if you have a night-light. Other reasons to keep a light on during sex:

- Betters photos
- Easier to locate obscure erogenous zones
- Deer won't get lonely

Mid-Sex Crises

Activity	Calories Burned
Coitus	45
Interruptus	74

Note: No calorie counts are available for minor mid-sex crises such as:

1. Surprise visit from meals-on-wheels
2. Forgetting to remove your barbecue apron

Positions (by Political Persuasion)

Because politics and sex are inextricably bound, many of our nation's largest elected officials asked what they might do in the privacy of their congressional district to keep their waistline under control. These positions have been pretested on candidates for public office:

Activity	Calories Burned
Republican, traditional ....31 (husband on top, wife under him)	
Republican, typical ....175 (wife on top, husband under indictment)	
Democrat ....99 (constantly changing positions)	
Conservative ....75 (one waiting to see what the other will do)	
Southern conservative ....140 (both emitting rebel yells)	
Ultra-conservative ....256 (back to back)	
Liberal, politically correct ....56 (woman on top, man looking up to her)	
Ultra-liberal, politically erect ....95 (both on top, but leaning to left)	
Extreme liberal (empathizing with the poor) ....22 (both trying to make ends meet)	
Irreconcilable political differences ....27 (man on left, woman on right)	

Two Bonus Positions

(For partners on their second marriage.)

Activity	Calories Burned
Man on top, woman suddenly realizing what was wrong with her first marriage	83
Woman on top, man under new management	145

Changing Positions

The monotony of having sex in the same position, night after night, year after year, may cause a relationship to stagnate or, worse, both partners to ferment. Weight loss benefits of this medium-impact event:

Activity	Calories Burned
In one fluid motion	.8
U-turn	.17
K-turn	.28
Forgetting to take your partner along	.159
Throwing your back out	.60
Falling off the bed	.20
Asking your partner to join you	.10

Safety tip: Satin sheets? Prevent skidding by wearing deck shoes.

Changing Locations

(To keep your sex life exciting.)

Activity	Calories Burned
Under the boardwalk:	
Atlantic City	.60
Kansas City	.160
On a chaise lounge	.28
On the floor:	
Carpeted	.32
Oak	.67
Tile	.90
In your dressing room	.52
In the Gap's dressing room	.105
In a daisy field	.33
Patrolled by a cranky bull	.148
In a shower stall	.55
Lying down	.83
On a picnic table	.41
Crushing the sandwiches of people already sitting there	.77
In the mattress section at Sears	.29

Exhaustion

In their zeal to lose weight, crash dieters spend too much time in bed. Some signs that you're overdoing it:

Activity	Calories Burned
Mailbox overflowing	.48
Leaves starting to turn	.67
Maid wants salary	.90
Another hike in postage rates	.124
Your grandchildren miss you	.13
Car impounded	.80
You're both starting to mildew	.210

Impotence

Should the male experience what sex therapists refer to as "down time," his partner, to put him at ease, should softly hum "Little Things Mean a Lot." Frequent causes:

Activity	Calories Burned
Frostbite	.24
Stagefright:	
Lights too bright	.17
Realtor showing the house	.44
Margarita abuse	.32
Partner is his boss	.28
Commanding officer	.50
Lodge brother	.94

When Bad Sex Happens to Good People

Activity	Calories Burned
Boredom	.11

Banishing the Blahs

Weight loss tips for couples who glance at their watch while making love or find themselves always doing it the same way, even during the mating season.

Activity	Calories Burned
Giving partner a haircut	.28
Talking dirty to each other	.16
In a British accent	1½
Using a vibrator	.18
If it's solar-powered	.173
Doing it in an unusual way:	
While watching the playoffs	.62
While driving with the top down	.78
Using an exotic condom:	
Glow-in-the-dark	.27
Fleece-lined	.34
Too tight	.371
Taking a bath together with partner's favorite toy:	
A rubber duck	.10
The au pair	.592

Mood-Wreckers

Activity	Calories Burned
Traffic noise	11
Partner leaning over to read an incoming fax	48
Housekeeper wants to know how many for dinner	19
Finding an earring that isn't yours	58
Or hers	74
Antiperspirant just quit	119
Wondering what to wear to work tomorrow	45
Cold sore	29
Trying to remember if you're wearing protection	88
Squeaking bed springs	11
Squeaking door hinge	56
Patter of little feet:	
Toddler	31
Roach	70

VI. Orgasm, and Beyond

"I told him that during orgasm, when I lose control, grab the sheets, bite my knuckles, scream, kick, writhe, moan, roll my eyes and shout 'Hallelujah!' I'm having fun, and not to call an exorcist."

—*Myrtle, visiting nurse*

Contrary to what weight loss experts advise, calories are burned not just by that funny face lovers make while in the throes of climax. A woman who has a difficult time just "letting go," even if her partner is still looking for a parking space, can burn significant calories. And a sensitive male will inevitably experience orgasm difficulties if his partner is showing vacation slides.

Things every lover should know about orgasm:

- You can't have too many.
- You can have too few.
- The ability to have them is a natural skill.
- The ability to give them is a marketable skill.
- A real one can't be faked.
- It wards off evil spirits, even if they brought a house gift.

Getting Close

A sign that you're approaching orgasm will be a feeling that this is not the best time to make a career decision. Additional indicators:

Activity	Calories Burned
Refusing to be hurried	15
If partner has a plane to catch	21
If you hear the garage door opening	55
(Add 200 calories if a voice says, "Honey, I'm home.")	
Shutting eyes	3
One at a time	6
Moaning	17
Short, shallow breaths (per breath)	4
Shaking	12
Shivering	25
Calling out partner's name:	
First	4
Last	10
Calling out someone else's name	47
Calling out your own name	65
If you're alone	3

Postponing Pleasure

If his partner has been crying, "Don't stop," for the past 40 minutes, the man approaching that "point of no return" can delay orgasm by focusing on something else.*

Activity	Calories Burned
Keg party	.10
MTV	.19
Why one should never fertilize perennials	.58
Pledge week	.38

*Recalling your first sexual experience can delay your orgasm for up to 3 months.

Note: Does thinking about baseball really work? Happily, sports fans, when asked during sex to imagine another baseball strike, were able to delay their orgasm for 2.6 weeks.

Orgasm

Activity	Calories Burned
Real	.49
Faked	.7
A blend	.65

Intensity Scale

No two orgasms are alike. Use the listing below to determine which one(s) you had.

Activity	Calories Burned
Finally exhaling	3
Bed slats break	35
Partner bites down on thumb	12
Yours	282
Oven mitt flies off	9
Trombones blow	17
Oboe toots	3½
Tsunami (only if your suite faces the beach)	60
Fireworks:	
Sparkler	9
Cherry bomb	58
Sudden sinus relief	17
Any out-of-body orgasm	95
Missing and presumed happy	140

Making Your Lover See Stars

Combining sex with astronomy, a pleasure-technique practiced by advanced lovers, promises to become one of the hot sexual topics of the '90s.

Activity	Calories Burned
Sighting a minor star:	
Betelguese	.42
Deneb	.57
Pee Wee Herman	.8
Sighting a major star*:	
Polaris	.63
Barbra Streisand	.90
Sighting a heavenly body:	
Venus	.32
Elvis	.200
Sighting a galaxy:	
The Milky Way	.77
The Mormon Tabernacle Choir	.153

*It is not unknown for lovers experiencing this level of pleasure to relive certain childhood memories such as the smell of Aunt Sadie's brisket or, even odder, suddenly recalling the words to "Why Must I Be a Teenager in Love?"

Simultaneous Orgasm

If you're:

Activity	Calories Burned
Competitors	.94
Conspirators	.66
Lucky	.2

Faking the Big O*

Activity	Calories Burned
Dramatically 31	
Without rehearsing 77	
Convincingly 145	

*Safe sex if you're alone.

Guilt

Confessing you fake it:

Activity	Calories Burned
To your best friend	15
To yourself	79
To your therapist:	
Jungian	10
Strict Freudian	14
Strict hairdresser	137
To your clergyman	17
Who happens to be your partner	90
To your personal shopper	3
(done only by partners with extreme guilt)	
To your personal trainer	50
To Geraldo	300

Time-Release Orgasm

If you experience it:

Activity	Calories Burned
The next morning	.44
During a power breakfast	.86
In church	.355
When the Novocain wears off	.155

How long should an orgasm last? With the right partner, experts suggest the length of *Die Meistersinger.* Others, more optimistic, insist that if cared for, an orgasm, like a Bonsai tree, can last for years, you need only replenish it with a partner.

The Wet Spot

Activity	Calories Burned
Avoiding it	.33
Lying in it	.57
(Add 90 calories if it's cold.)	
Sinking in it	.151

Point of Sexual Etiquette

Feminists may quibble, but unless it's from her moisturizer, gallantry dictates that the male partner lie in any wet spot caused by:

- Him
- Flop sweat
- The juicy details
- A leaky roof
- Bird droppings*

*Al fresco sex only.

Sexual Miracles

Remarkable high-calorie events that occur when the chemistry between two lovers is right.

Activity	Calories Burned
Your first climax	.19
With a partner	.155
Making love twice in one week	.75
One night	.149
One bed	.18
After 25 years of marriage	.600
The earth moved	.137
The earth quaked (Pacific Coast only)	.244

Rhythm Methods

(Music to make love to.)

Activity	Calories Burned
Soul	.27
Big band	.36
Rap:	
Black	.194
White	.6
Lite FM	.2¼
On an elevator	.45
(Add 1 calorie if partner tapping foot.)	
Rock	.22
Roll	.23
Texas swing	.55
Heavy metal	.68
Sheet metal	.5
Tango	.73
With a rose clamped between your teeth	.87
Reggae*	.99

*Not recommended for couples with a frail bed.

Differing Sex Drives

A problem if you want sex three times weekly and your partner wants it only on Father's Day.

Activity	Calories Burned
Your partner wants sex every night	195
With you	274
With someone just like you	8
You want sex in the morning	19
Your partner likes it at night	28
Compromising	66
(making love at 4:25 A.M.)	
You don't care if you ever have sex again	2
You just go through the motions	3
You've pushed the beds apart	28
You're sleeping in the guest room	36
With a guest	100

VII. Afterplay

This is where ordinary sex manuals end, the authors unaware that ecstasy and, if you have energy left, weight loss are just beginning. You are, after all, working out with the one you love—exhaustion, double vision and pleading for pasta primavera are not uncommon. Nobody said that recovering from sex would be easy. In this section, you'll learn the benefits of not instantly falling asleep (burns only 4 calories and could make your partner do something hostile, like sneak out of bed and withdraw all your money from an ATM machine). The recovery table below, prepared by a Surgeon General, will interest those affected by Post-Lovemaking Stress Syndrome, a sign of which will be a partner's valiant but unsuccessful attempt to explain the popularity of *Forrest Gump*.

After sex, a lover should be able to:	In:
Roll over and fall asleep	.2 seconds
Grant an encore	.100 minutes
Operate heavy machinery (an automobile)	.10 minutes
The bathroom light switch	.5 minutes
A Craftmatic adjustable bed	.25 minutes
Be creative:	
Write a thank-you note	.6 minutes
Donate sperm	.7 hours
Flawlessly accessorize a new fall wardrobe	.2–3 hours
Check the clock to see where the time went	.4 minutes
Check the scale to see where the weight went	.7 minutes

If Sex Was Good

Activity	Calories Burned
Walking on air	4

If Sex Was Bad

Activity	Calories Burned
Walking on thin ice 111	

Encore

Activity	Calories Burned
If she's ready 257
But he's not 6

Weight Loss Bonus #2

Activity	Calories Burned
Feeling numb 4	
Feeling sticky 35	
Telling your partner how wonderful it was 10	
If partner already asleep 19	
But grinning 42	
Wondering if you made your partner's A-list 31	
Apologizing for taking so long 17	
Apologizing for not taking long enough 56	

Afterglow

Always experienced by contented couples. The wattage of each partner's "glow" is determined by the quality of lovemaking. A shiny forehead, particularly on one normally afflicted with dry skin, is the criterion most often cited by dermatologists. Lovers who actually made the earth move will babble and should be stabilized with tea and toast.

Activity	Calories Burned
Feeling at peace with the world	12
With your pending tax audit	17
With the fact that you forgot to use protection	231
Feeling like a god	40
A goddess	41
A cigarette	15
A cigar	30
Experiencing celestial bliss	28
Waving to the Space Shuttle	55
Floating back to earth	11
Missing it	166

Rewarding Your Lover

Assorted gifts for the lover who makes you feel special.

Activity	Calories Burned
Giving him a sponge bath	66
Letting her use the bathroom first	11
A weekend in London	269
A night in Enid, Oklahoma	3
Moving her piano	104
Up four flights of stairs	739
Cleaning out his refrigerator	46
His garage	113
The trunk of his car	526
Giving her flowers that you picked yourself	24
Illegally	80
Candy (Godiva)	78
Candy (exotic dancer)	166
More closet space	49
Upgrading partner	60
(from side dish to main dish)	

Pillow Talk

Lovers who are not comatose should utter something, even a sound bite, to indicate that sex was wonderful.

Activity	Calories Burned
Post-lovemaking statements 20	

Examples:

"What kept you?"

"I should be getting home, my plants will be wondering where I am."

"I couldn't have done it without you."

"Do you take plastic?"
(actors in Hollywood who prefer anonymous sex only)

"Your turn to let the dog out."

"We're thinner!"

"I never did that with my husband."

"Do you think the photos will come out?"

"It's been so long since I've been with a man."

"Me, too."

Things to Be Happy About After Sex

(Rewards, aside from weight loss and the disappearance of liver spots, for dieters to rejoice about.)

Activity	Calories Burned
You're blushing	.5
Your urologist was wrong	.8
Your cholesterol fell	.20
Your ex had the kids	.12
The phone didn't ring	.25
The baby kept its promise not to cry	.43
Your in-laws didn't show up	.75
He asked for your hand	.50
To move a credenza	.6
Your tan didn't rub off	.16
You're not the one lying in the wet spot	.100

Things to Be Sad About After Sex

Activity	Calories Burned
It's over	77
Partner isn't staying the night	66
And it's her apartment	158

Regaining Your Composure

Some typical after-sex activities:

Activity	Calories Burned
Administering first aid for stubble burn:	
From his cheeks	.22
From her legs	.85
Wondering if you're still chaste	.3
Looking to see	.25
Sharing a cigarette	.7
The nicotine patch	.15
Blowing out the candles	.8
Whining about secondhand smoke	.14
Righting the nightstand	.26
Carving your initials on his headboard	.29
Autographing her sheets	.18
Returning downstairs to your guests	.44

Breakfast in Bed

A post-lovemaking ritual for which gourmets counsel heart-healthy fare—juice, Wheaties, eggs Benedict with skim milk and herbal tea—unless you're pressed for time. Then a creamsicle will do.

Activity	Calories Burned
Plumping the pillows	.17
Positioning the breakfast tray	.14
If you're still having sex	.55
Removing the tea cozy	.3
If partner wearing it as a party hat	.29
Cutting partner's sausage into bite-size pieces	.22
Very carefully	.40
Peeling a grape (an ultra-romantic gesture)	.12
If you bite your nails	.31
Feeding each other scrambled eggs	.22
Without utensils	.88
More sex:*	
On a full stomach	.65
On your partner's stomach	.144

*A brunch substitute.

Thanking Partner for a Wonderful Night

Even if Hallmark had a card for this, you wouldn't want it. Shun prepackaged sentiment and express your own feelings, no matter how risqué.* If you have writer's block, stimulate the creative juices by pressing the bed sheets to your bosom. (*Intimacy tip:* Unless you're calligraphically challenged, your card should be handwritten.)

Activity	Calories Burned
Sending an intimate note:	
By mail	9
By carrier pigeon	20
If it dawdles	63
Signing your note "Guess who?"	5
If partner has no idea who it's from	200
Calling instead	15
From work	19
With boss standing 3 feet away	28
Sending a fax	18
If it falls into the wrong hands	90

*With an easy-to-shock partner, a simple line like "Marry me" is appropriate.

Parting from Each Other

After a night of romance, facing the morning is not an easy task, particularly if it's a workday and you hate your job.

Activity	Calories Burned
Leaving a nice warm bed:	
If you're a morning person 10	
If you're a night person 623	
And you're wrapped around each other 750	
Wondering if your partner has an extra toothbrush 6	
Wondering if you can get away with wearing the same outfit to work 60	

Note for Commuters

Increase all calorie counts:

By:	If:
2%	You take the train
5%	You carpool
8%	You loathe the other passengers
27%	You go by subway

VIII. Supplementary Pleasures

Not all of the following activities occur during the normal course of sexual events. They do, however, offer weight loss opportunities, and this might be the perfect time to try something other than covering the bird cage, setting the alarm and engaging in the missionary position for 7.3 minutes (or 7.3 seconds if it's his busy season). Extra calories, for example, will be burned by lovers whose erotic fantasy consists of something atypical, like unlimited entrée to designer showrooms. A partner who commences foreplay by crying himself to sleep can cause his startled partner to shed significant pounds. And adventurous couples, even if they don't use little booster rockets, will finally understand why, after an intense night of lovemaking, they weigh only 17 pounds and can't see over the steering wheel.

Note: If you have an extra moment, this is the time to seek out that elusive G-spot, usually found on people who are extra-ticklish. You know you've found it if your partner:

- Kicks the covers off the bed
- Begins moaning in Dutch

Senior Sex

Activity	Calories Burned
Sex in your Winnebago 42	
If it doesn't have tinted windows ....158 *(20-calorie bonus if the excitement makes your "Wishin' I was fishin' " bumper sticker fall off)*	
Apologizing for holding up traffic 25	

> *Note:* Instead of bee pollen, lovers over 50 who decide not to age turn to sex.* Not only does it give extra meaning to the phrase "Early Bird Special," but, as one 57-year-old explained, "It keeps my boyfriend's prostate humming right along." (Many seniors, alas, decline sex, believing it will make them look younger than they really are and force them, when taking public transportation, to pay full fare.)

*In his landmark study, "Guano: Why Bats Fear Their Own Sexuality," Dr. Babcock Dingly, holder of the chair that doesn't wobble at Heidi's Bible College, concluded that couples over 60 who engage in vigorous sex five or more times weekly are least likely to complain that their children never call.

Watching Adult Movies*

Activity	Calories Burned
In a theater	49
If you're spotted by someone from the office	200
In the privacy of your bedroom	30
Rental	45
Pay-Per-View	14
Constantly pressing the freeze-frame button	6
Getting aroused	49
Because of what the actors are doing	77
Because you recognize your spouse	255

Sending Your Lover to Rent an Adult Movie

Activity	Calories Burned
If he returns with *Debbie Does Dallas*	133
With *Jurassic Park*	2

*A low-impact activity for lovers intent on exploring their sexuality.

Lovers' Quarrels*

Arguments over:

Activity	Calories Burned
Money	.35
How high to set the air conditioner	.127
Sex	.30
We don't do it enough	.45
We don't do it, period	.163
Whose turn it is to feed the baby	.33
Whose turn it is to feed the weekend guest	.100
Prayer in school	.24
Prayer in the bedroom	.84
Custody:	
For your share of the covers	.12
For the non-lumpy side of the mattress	.16
For the good side of the bed (closest to the bathroom)	.24

*Between loving couples, the occasional fight can make sex even better (unless it's over a dent in the new BMW).

Making Up

Activity	Calories Burned
Over dinner	.23
In bed	.78
For lost time	.141

Group Therapy

Activity	Calories Burned
A threesome:	
Two men, one woman .... .245	
One man, two women .... .245	
If he's not included .... .327	

A foursome (you and your partner in front of a mirror) ...... .85

Gay Sex

Activity	Calories Burned
Coming out of the closet	.56
Not liking what you see	.17
Going back in	.84

Sex in the Workplace

Activity	Calories Burned
On company time 98	

On company furniture:
In the mailroom 66	
In the boardroom 42	
In the utility room 125	

The Nooner

Activity	Calories Burned
Parking vehicle so it can't be seen from the road	.37
Mazda Miata	.4
Tractor trailer	.109
Checking into motel	.8
Demanding corporate rate	.25
Slowly undressing	.14
If motel charges by the hour	.62
Talking business in bed	.5
Because it gets you excited	.11
So you can write off the motel room	.45
Safe sex (swearing each other to secrecy)	.30
Safer sex (making sure no one sees you leaving)	.74

Advantages of daytime lovemaking:

1. It's easier to find a vacant motel room.
2. The stores are still open. If sex was disappointing, you can still go shopping.

Phone Sex

Those few calories that dialing a 900 number burn may not seem worth it, but this is the ultimate in safe sex— except when your partner sees the phone bill.*

Activity	Calories Burned
Calling from home	.9
On a party line	.35
Calling from work	.17
On a speaker phone	.35
Conference call	.52
Using a pay phone	.24
That has call waiting	.77
Using your car phone	.22
While trying to parallel park	.80
If you recognize the voice on the other end	.40
If that voice recognizes you	.180

*Decrease all calorie counts by 10% if you think you're actually speaking to the people you see on your TV screen.

Cybersex

For those who fear intimacy, the safest sex of all—unless it's the CIA on the Internet.

Activity	Calories Burned
Sitting down at computer	4
Removing dustcover	6
If computer's modest	20
Going online	2
Finding E-mail from a friend	8
From "Brandy"	75
Making certain you're alone	9
Transmitting	18
If mouse jams	35
If mouse wants to participate	97
Receiving	7
If you're offended by what you see	33
And outraged by poor picture quality	85
Downloading	6
Signing off	3
Sighing off	2
Rolling over and falling asleep	10

IX. Sex-Related Stress

Those who fear regaining the pounds they've shed need not worry. This is the maintenance part of your diet—those during-sex glitches that happen to everyone and, if they're sufficiently disastrous, trim all but the most unyielding fat deposits. For any of the events below, give yourself only 5 calories; they are but minor during-sex inconveniences. Major problems are covered in the following pages.

- Jehovah's witnesses peering through bedroom window, asking if you've been saved.
- Couple next-door sound like they're having more fun than you (Howard Johnson motels only).
- Hide-a-bed suddenly closes (add 2 calories if you keep going).
- Ginseng repeating.
- Tabloid reporters closing in.

When the Unthinkable Happens

Some common during-sex emergencies, other than hecklers, that may threaten the magic mood. The remedies are a) an understanding partner, and b) keep going no matter what.

Activity	Calories Burned
Cramp:	
Leg	11
Menstrual	137
Chafed elbows	19
(Caused by making love on bargain sheets. Professional lovers swear by Corn Huskers Lotion.)	
Torn ligament	66
(Caused by attempting intercourse in the back-to-back position.)	
Acid flashback	45
To the sixties	189
Chest pains caused by:	
Your heart	29
His medals	90
Bedsores	27
Rope burns	99

Overcoming Adversity

The truly unselfish person can rise above personal circumstances and say "Yes" willingly, even joyfully when his or her partner wants to make love. A sampling of weight lost when pleasing your partner under less-than-ideal circumstances:

Activity	Calories Burned
You have a headache:	
Regular	.20
Migraine	.65
FBI at the door	.94
You just had a manicure	.11
And your nails are still wet	.55
Your stock portfolio's down	.47
Your guests will arrive any minute	.66
You're 8½ months pregnant	.91
You're in labor	.300

Having an Affair

Infidelity is not an approved way to burn calories, and it's certainly not what we'd consider "safe" sex if your partner's spouse collects deer rifles. Those who stray, however, still have a right to determine for themselves whether, weight-loss-wise, fooling around is worth it.

Activity	Calories Burned
Coming home with lipstick on your collar	.39
On your face	.65
Somewhere else	.372
If your spouse is suspicious	.90
Dusts you for fingerprints	.206
Explaining it's your:	
New barber	.45
New secretary	.96
New mistress	.245
Mid-life crisis	.300
Lying	.18
If you're not good at it	.70

Getting Caught

Activity	Calories Burned
Denying everything	.68
Despite the photos	.200

Sexual Harassment

Activity	Calories Burned
Leaving the seat up	.80

Impure Acts

Unless you're a bachelor, strict theologians consider self-abuse a sin. Enlightened experts, on the other hand, say it's healthy, unless one's erotic fantasy happens to be a cassette of the Congressional Soybean Caucus singing torch songs.

Activity	Calories Burned
Lying there, letting yourself do all the work	47
Going blind	5
Going insane	7

Sex with Animals

(An environmentally aware lover never takes advantage of endangered species.)

Activity	Calories Burned
A frog	17
With bedroom eyes	39
A dark horse	36
A teddy bear	83
Stuffed	12
A tiger	70
A tigress	128
Any party animal	77
Wearing a lampshade	110
A Newt	6

Things Often Said After Sex with an Animal

Activity	Calories Burned
"Polly want a cracker."	18

S & M

Mistress Bambi, dominatrix-in-waiting to the Senate, asserts that even more calories are burned when a partner uses Miracle Whip.

Activity	Calories Burned
S	.67
M	.55
If both partners are dominant	.134
If both partners are sissies	.8
Bickering over who gets to wear the slave bracelet	.200
Ordering partner to kiss your feet	.19¼
Chew through your nylons	.45
Spanking with a popsicle stick	.14
Making your partner watch the Miss Universe Pageant	.23
Searching for keys to:	
The car	.10
The handcuffs	.19

Cross-Dressing

Activity	Calories Burned
If he's prettier than you	186

Jealousy

A normal human emotion that induces extra-high weight loss if it prevents an insecure partner from keeping solids down.

Activity	Calories Burned
Catching partner flirting with:	
The waitress	.17
The waiter	.37
The lamb chop	.54
Obsessing over lover's past	.29
If there are notches on her bedpost	.77
Lover taking phone calls during sex	.44
(Add 63 calories if you're not allowed to say hello.)	
Receiving less affection from lover than:	
Her cat	.62
His golf partner	.100
Catching partner in bed with another woman	.80
Another man	.122
Both	.500
Observing spouse leaving a motel room	.9
And you know he's not the room clerk	.278
Partner gives you a ticket to Rome	.41
One way	.253

The Second Honeymoon

Couples returning to Bermuda or Paris with their same spouse of 30 years may use the previous sections of this book. Increase all calorie counts by 10%, however, if sex has gotten better and to allow for inflation. The calorie counts below are for partners on their second marriage.

Activity	Calories Burned
Older man, younger wife:	
If he married her for love	.87
If she married him for money	.5
Older man, trophy wife	.372
Older woman, younger husband	.106
Older woman, much younger husband:	
Boy toy	.178
Action toy	.400

When Sex Tapers Off

Activity	Calories Burned
Memories 52	

11 Uses for an Ex-Lover
(Should things not work out.)

1. Good friend
2. Doorstop
3. Palimony
4. Recipe tester
5. Organ donor
6. Furniture mover
7. Fourth for bridge
8. Dog walker
9. Stocking stuffer
10. Sex (strictly platonic)
11. Trade-in

X. Family Values

For dieting couples, the weight loss benefits of trying to start a family are immense, particularly if one partner (the male, for example) has an iffy sperm count (+6) and asks, after every orgasm, "Do you think you got pregnant this time?" Additionally, because you're having sex for procreation rather than pleasure, suppressing moans of pleasure and keeping a straight face during intercourse burn extra calories.

Also contributing to weight loss are related activities such as trying to decide whether to use his ex as a midwife (155 calories), worrying whether you can really afford to start a family (296 calories, but only 3½ calories if in-laws have established a college trust fund) and wondering whose parents will make better baby-sitters (the ones who have the most patience and the fewest breakable knickknacks).

Note: Once pregnancy occurs, and in order to minimize weight gain, sex should continue so long as you a) heed the advice of your practitioner, and b) can find a comfortable position.

Reasons for Starting a Family

Activity	Calories Burned
You both want children	36
You owe it to the world	97
You hope it'll improve your marriage	8
Your biological clock is ticking:	
Windup	14
Quartz	20
Egg timer	35
Too many calories in birth-control pills	10
Your parents are eager to become grandparents	18
Your in-laws own a toy store	79
You need an heir	41
You need a tax deduction	82
You're out of condoms	3

Trying to Conceive

Unfortunately, extra-fertile couples burn negligible calories, unless they forget to remove the condom.

Activity	Calories Burned

Simplified Version

Glint in partner's eye	6
Undressing	17
Sex	85
Luck (getting pregnant on first try)	42

Complicated Version

Calculating optimal times	55
If you're poor at math	177
Writing checks to fertility centers	31
Trying to get your money back	500
Trying and trying:	
For her	22
For him	195
For the bed	390
Giving a sperm sample	66
Missing the cup	159

Pregnancy Test—Positive

Announcing to your family that you're pregnant burns a mere 8 calories (or 22 if you call collect). It's that special, intimate moment, when you tell the father-to-be, that really consumes calories.

Activity	Calories Burned
Telling him the good news	.33
If he replies:	
"Darling, that's wonderful."	.27
"Can't this wait until halftime?"	.50
"Is it mine?"	.71
"Is it yours?"	.229
Rejoicing	.55
Dancing around the room with spouse	.141
With anonymous donor	.600
With test tube	.5
Ignoring government warning	.22
(celebrating with a bottle of Dom Pérignon)	

Morning Sickness

Activity	Calories Burned
Holding her head	8
Holding the bucket	12
If he's squeamish	39

Midnight Cravings (Hers)*

Activity	Calories Burned
Gatorade	.6
Pickles	.14
With ice cream	.88
Any exotic nosh	.47
Niçoise Cornish Hen Salad	.63
Tacos en Gelée	.81
Rice Pudding on a Bed of Leeks	.215

*Check first with your doctor.

Point of Father-to-Be Etiquette

To instantly satisfy his wife's culinary desires, the considerate husband keeps a hot plate and little refrigerator on his side of the bed.

Midnight Cravings (His)

Activity	Calories Burned
Sex 700	

Sex Substitutes

Because it's sometimes difficult to feel sexy with a) a backache, b) nausea, and c) flatulence, we present the following nearly-as-good alternates:

Activity	Calories Burned
Counting the loot from the baby shower	.31
Multiple checkups	.77
Buying a crib	.26

Wondering if you'll ever again:
    Feel thin
    Fit into pedal pushers
	
	.10
	.29

Buying a baseball glove (suggests a presumptuous father-to-be)	.40
Taking bids on "It's a boy/girl" cigars	.25
Watching your breasts enlarge	.60
Recalling how they got this way	.19

Giving Birth

Activity	Calories Burned
Contractions:	
For her (per contraction)	.22
For him (per contraction)	.3
If he panics	.77
Driving to the hospital	.52
Labor	1,381
Pacing	1,381
The delivery	.772
With husband assisting:*	
Offering encouragement	15
(wiping her head and yelling, "Push!")	
Trying to hold the minicam steady	.31
Fainting	.500
Thanking the stork	.10

*20-calorie bonus if he's getting on the obstetrician's nerves.

Getting to Know Baby

Activity	Calories Burned
Deciding who baby looks like	41
As it's emerging from the womb	238

Trying to get baby's attention through nursery window:	
Shaking a rattle	5
Waving a Yale pennant	7
Shouting	11
If it's the wrong baby	52

Deciding who to name baby after	56
Changing your mind	19
Twice	24
Five times	73
Erasing the ink on the birth certificate	92

Waiting to Resume Sex

Activity	Calories Burned
Until you get home from the hospital	266
Until you pay off the hospital	2,830
Until you decide who baby most resembles	123
Until baby's first smile	90
Until baby's first tooth	159
Until you're ready for the next baby	114
Until baby goes off to college	372

Point of Sexual Etiquette

Who gets up in the middle of the night to feed baby? If baby is nursing, the wife. Etiquette dictates, however, that the husband, in sympathy, remain fully awake until she returns to bed. If it isn't nursing, baby is fed by the partner who refrained, during sex, from saying, "Shhh, we'll wake the baby."

About the Author

Richard Smith weighs even less today than he did in 1978, when he wrote the original, best-selling *Dieter's Guide*.